Contents

In their own words
Look for these boxes to find inspirational quotes from the kids featured in this book and other famous people who made a difference.

Kids who made a difference

These boxes tell you stories about kids who have done great things to make the world a better place, both now and in the past.

Top tips

Search for these boxes for quick facts about how you can make a difference.

Some words in the book are in bold, **like this**. You can find out what they mean by looking in the glossary.

So many ways to help

Helping others is fun. It is rewarding, too. Young people help others every day, often beginning by helping at home. Perhaps you help by doing the laundry, preparing meals, or looking after younger brothers and sisters.

Many young people reach out to their neighbours. Simple acts of kindness make a big difference. Older people may need help doing errands or caring for their gardens. They may be lonely. Just waving and saying "hello" can make a difference.

Keeping your neighbourhood safe is important, too. Something as simple as reporting broken glass in a play area may prevent other children from getting hurt. Being a good example to younger children is also helpful.

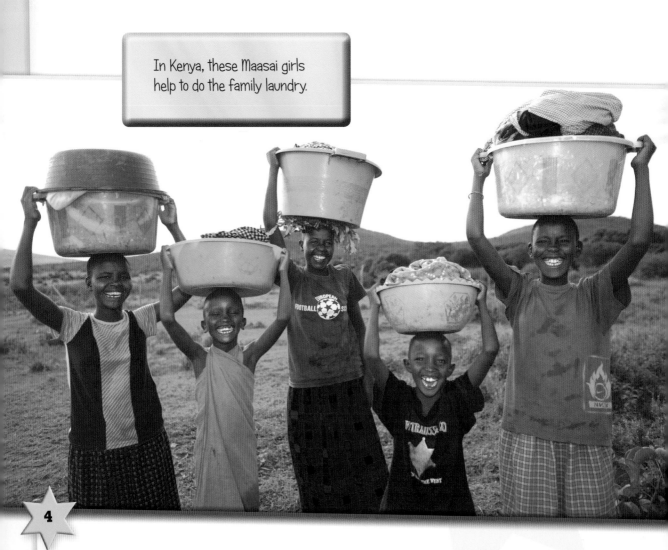

In Kenya, these Maasai girls help to do the family laundry.

These children are working with a charity to prepare meals for needy families in Michigan, USA.

Kids who made a difference

Jimmy Carter began helping out on his father's farm when he was only five or six by carrying drinking water to the farm workers. When he was older, he helped care for the animals and protect the cotton crop from insects. Helping others became Jimmy Carter's lifelong goal. He was president of the United States from 1977 to 1981. Later, he set up the Carter Center, an organization that helps fight disease and hunger in Africa and Asia.

In their own words

Aesop, a storyteller in ancient Greece, wrote a fable called The Lion and the Mouse. The **moral** of the story is, "No act of kindness, no matter how small, is ever wasted."

Helping the community

Young people can help others by working with organizations such as Cancer Research UK, children's hospitals, or the Red Cross. Groups such as the Boy Scouts, Girl Guides, and other clubs often take part in **community service projects**.

Sometimes, young people pitch in to help their communities at times of crisis. During floods, such as the one in Fargo, North Dakota, USA, schoolchildren played a major role in helping to build **dykes** to hold back floodwaters. Younger children helped fill sandbags and passed out water and food to workers. Everyone pulled together to save the community. After a disaster, such as a flood, hurricane, or tornado, young people may also help with the clean-up.

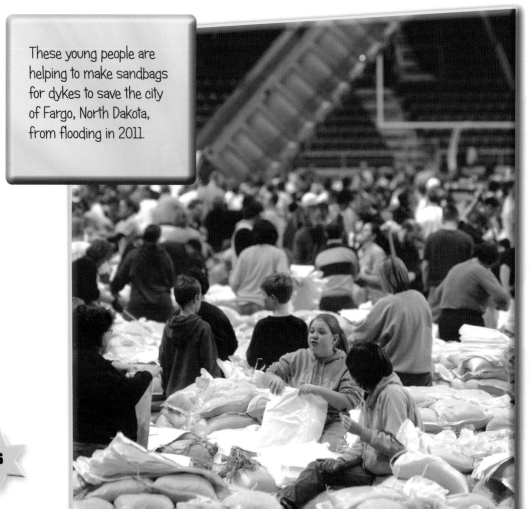

These young people are helping to make sandbags for dykes to save the city of Fargo, North Dakota, from flooding in 2011.

These teenagers are recycling aluminium cans.

Recycling

In Cyprus, an island in the Mediterranean Sea, teenagers help others through a project called Cans for Kids. They sort out aluminium cans at a **recycling** centre. Companies buy the recycled aluminium, and Cans for Kids uses the money to purchase medical equipment for a children's hospital. The teenagers are helping the environment as well as sick children.

Top tips

Some projects, such as recycling, need everyone's help. Recycling and picking up litter help the entire community. Find out about recycling projects in your community. If there is an aluminium can or plastic bottle recycling project that pays for recycled items, you can donate the money you earn to your favourite cause.

School projects

Many schools hold **fundraising** events to help others. In the United Kingdom, some schools participate in Red Nose Day, **sponsored** by the **charity** Comic Relief. Students do "something funny for money". They may put on a talent show or wear silly costumes or a red nose to school for a day. They raise money by charging admission or asking people to sponsor them. The money supports those in need throughout the UK and in Africa.

There are dozens of ways to help. Some take only a few minutes while others require hours of effort. Students around the world entertain people in hospitals or nursing homes. They help younger children with schoolwork or do errands or gardening work for elderly neighbours.

In their own words

Doctor and thinker William James (1842–1910) had an outlook on life that we can still learn from today. He said, "act as if what you do makes a difference. It does."

Helping Haiti

Many schools have raised money to help the victims of the 2010 earthquake in the Caribbean nation of Haiti. At one New York City high school, students paid a fee to play basketball against their teachers. They sent the money to help rebuild Haiti.

This schoolgirl is taking part in a lunch club for the elderly in Chelmsford, Essex.

Tackling big problems

While many children help in their homes, schools, and neighbourhoods, some young people have taken helping others a step further. They have learned new skills like **first aid** or gardening in order to help their neighbours. Others are making a difference by tackling serious problems like hunger, child labour, or water shortages in faraway places. Read on to meet some of these amazing kids.

Top tips

Check to see if your school supports a particular charity. If so, get involved. If not, get together with friends and suggest a project to your headteacher. Make sure to do your research first. It is best to have a workable plan before you begin.

Matt Pearce: saving lives

Matt Pearce, aged 15, was delivering newspapers when he noticed that one of his regular customers had left her door wide open. Matt looked inside to see if everything was all right. He found Joan Robson, an 84-year-old woman, clinging to the doorframe. Her speech was slurred.

"I was studying first aid in school and I recognized her **symptoms**," Matt said. "I thought it was a stroke straight away." A stroke occurs when the blood flow to the brain is interrupted or reduced. Symptoms include trouble walking and talking, headaches, blurred vision, or numbness on one side of the body or face. Strokes may cause brain damage or even death. Prompt medical treatment reduces the risk of death and brain damage.

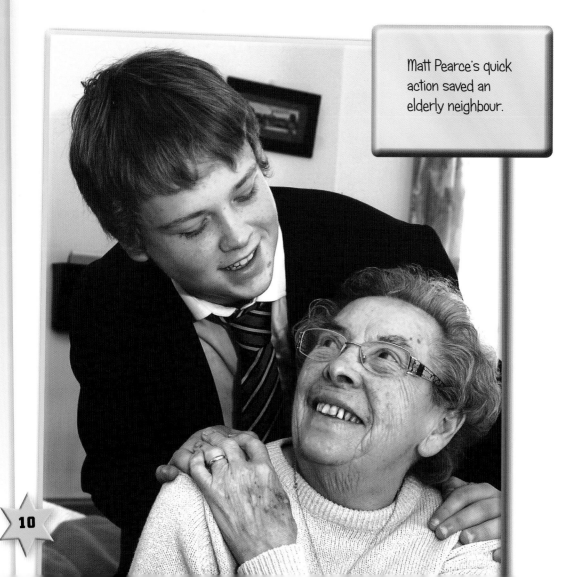

Matt Pearce's quick action saved an elderly neighbour.

Matt helped Mrs Robson to a seat and promised not to leave her alone. Then he called an ambulance. When it arrived, he helped the **paramedics** care for Mrs Robson. Matt later visited her in hospital. She recovered completely, thanks to Matt's quick response.

In their own words

When interviewed by the local newspaper, Matt Pearce said, "I am not a hero, I was just helping out. I like helping the people on my round however I can."

Matt lives in Longlevens, Gloucester in southern England.

In their own words

Mother Teresa, a Catholic **nun**, spent her life helping the poor and ill in India. She once said, "Help one person at a time, and always start with the person nearest you."

Helping again

A few days later, Matt and a friend were walking along a nearby street. Matt noticed a man sitting on the ground. Later Matt described the situation: "His speech started to slur, too, and I thought he was having a stroke . . . so I called the ambulance again." Thanks to Matt's quick response, the man received the medical care he needed.

Heart attack

Dionne Burns took a Red Cross first aid class in her hometown of Glasgow, Scotland. After she completed the class, she volunteered to help out at a 4-kilometre (2.5-mile) race. One of the runners, Ian Kennedy, suffered a heart attack at the finish line, and he stopped breathing. Dionne knew exactly what to do. She called for help, and then she used a special lifesaving machine to shock his heart. He started breathing again and, within a short time, paramedics arrived and took over. Dionne's training and her quick action saved Ian's life.

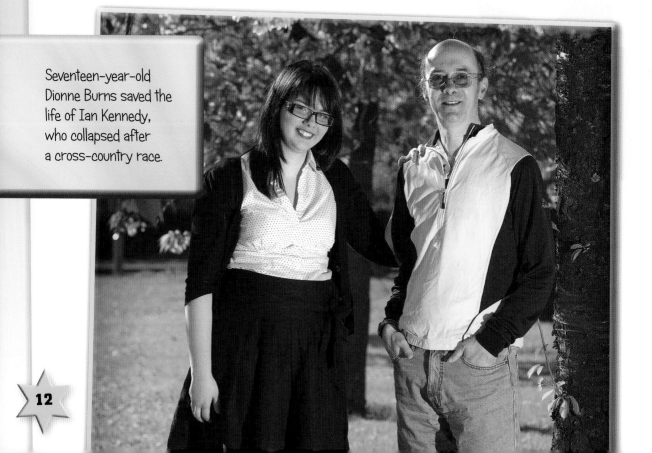

Seventeen-year-old Dionne Burns saved the life of Ian Kennedy, who collapsed after a cross-country race.

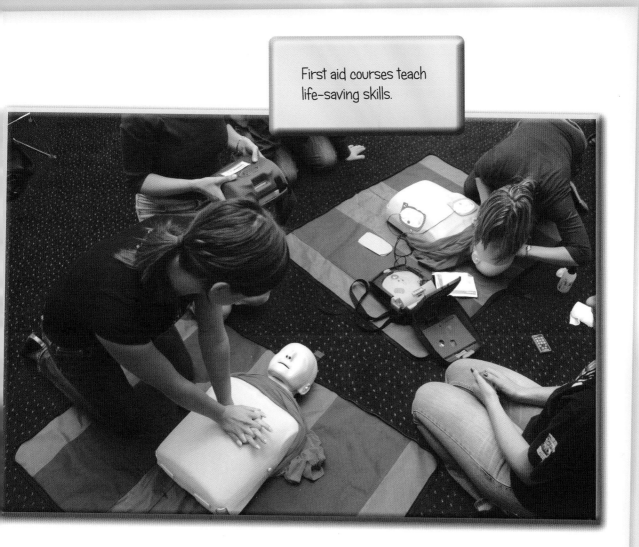

First aid courses teach life-saving skills.

The Red Cross and St John Ambulance both offer a variety of first aid courses for young people and adults. Some courses teach workplace and school safety. Others teach people how to respond to common accidents, as well as to life-threatening emergencies such as strokes or heart attacks. The Red Cross also offers babysitting courses to prepare young people to care for younger children.

Top tips

Take a first aid or water safety course. You'll not only help yourself, but you may have the opportunity to help someone else, too.

13

Screaming for help

It is important to be **observant**. Matt Pearce noticed something was wrong, so he called for help. Jared Vigil, of Louisville, Colorado in the United States didn't see a problem; he heard one. On 6 February 2008, 14-year-old Jared heard screaming on his way home from school. He wasn't sure if it was an animal or a person, so he stopped and looked around. That's when he realized that his neighbour, Connie Ostwald, had fallen into an icy pond. Jared called the emergency services, then he adjusted the straps on his backpack and used it to pull the woman out of the freezing water.

Top tips

Make sure everyone knows how to call for help. Even young children can call 999 in an emergency.

Staying safe

Matt, Dionne, and Jared did everything right. As soon as they realized that someone was in trouble, they called for help. It is important to let others know there is a problem as quickly as possible. Paramedics, firefighters, and police have the training and equipment to help in emergencies.

These kids also knew that the first rule in rescue is personal safety. An injured rescuer can't help anyone else. That's why Jared stayed safely on dry land. Wading into the icy water would have been dangerous.

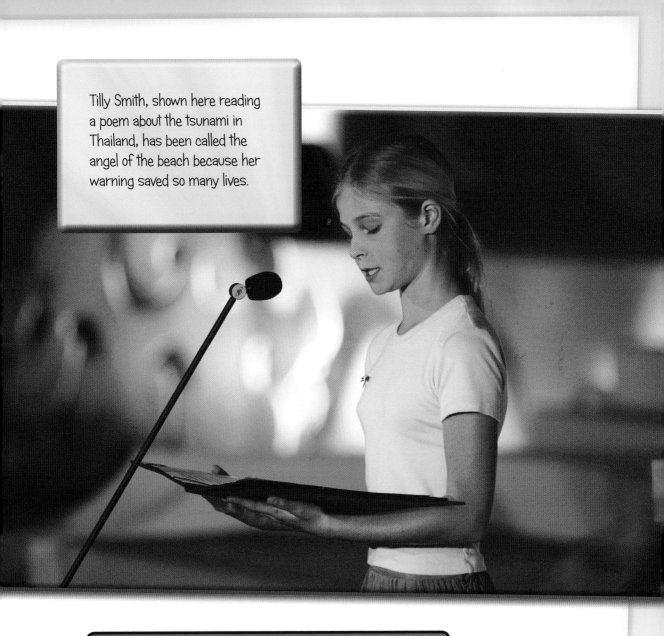

Tilly Smith, shown here reading a poem about the tsunami in Thailand, has been called the angel of the beach because her warning saved so many lives.

Kids who made a difference

British schoolgirl Tilly Smith, aged 10, travelled to Thailand with her family in December 2004. Tilly, who had just studied **tsunamis** at school, noticed the early warning signs on the beach. She warned everyone to run for safety. Her warning saved more than 100 tourists from the killer wave.

Katie Stagliano: feeding the hungry

Katie Stagliano's dream of helping others began with a cabbage seedling. Every child in her class received one seedling thanks to a scheme in her school that gives cabbage plants to children in third grade (year 4). Katie planted her seedling in her garden. She watered it and fed it plant food to make it grow well. Katie's grandfather helped her build a sturdy wire cage around the cabbage plant to protect it from deer. The cabbage grew … and grew … and grew. It eventually weighed in at 18 kilograms (40 pounds)!

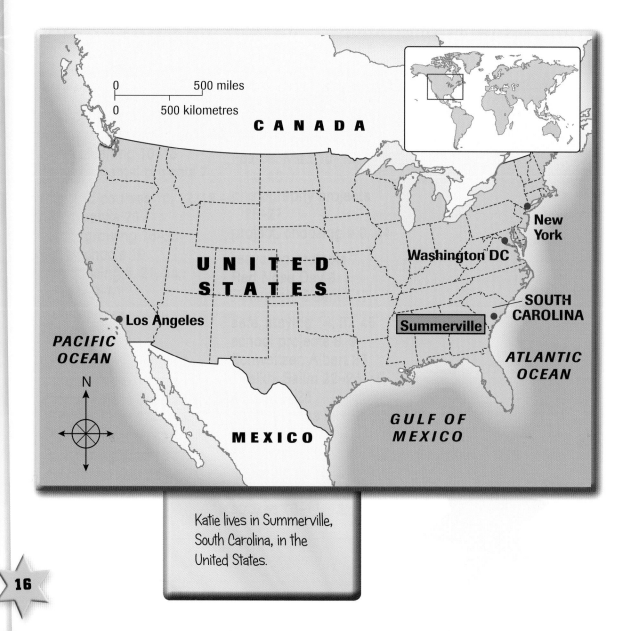

Katie lives in Summerville, South Carolina, in the United States.

A growing idea

Katie wanted to do something special with her cabbage. Her mother contacted Fields to Families, an organization that helps farmers get crops to groups that feed the hungry. They suggested that Katie give the cabbage to Tri County Family Ministries, a local **soup kitchen**.

The soup kitchen eagerly accepted Katie's gift. That one cabbage, along with some ham and rice, fed 250 hungry people. Katie went to the soup kitchen and helped serve the meal. When she saw how much good one cabbage could do, Katie decided to grow a vegetable garden to help feed people in need. Katie began planning. She wanted to create a big garden and give away the vegetables.

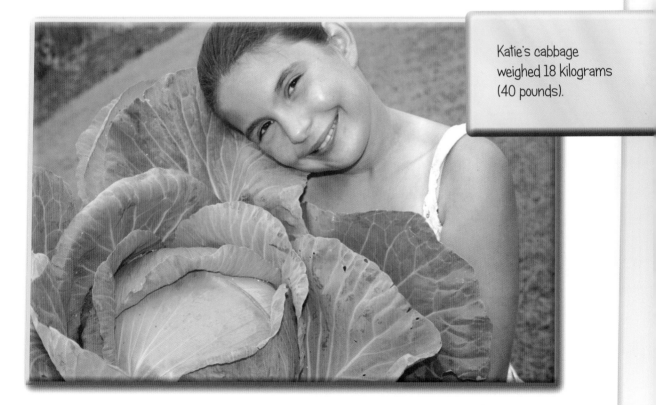

Katie's cabbage weighed 18 kilograms (40 pounds).

In their own words
Eleanor Roosevelt, **First Lady** of the United States from 1933 to 1945, was an American author, **diplomat**, and **humanitarian**. She once said: "It is not fair to ask others [to do] what you are unwilling to do yourself."

Growing the project

The next summer, Katie grew more vegetables. She gave her harvest to people in need. She wanted to do more, but seeds and equipment are expensive. Family, friends, and classmates helped. So did community organizations, seed companies, and local farmers.

In 2009, Katie began her own **non-profit organization**, Katie's Krops. She developed a website to explain her project and to encourage others to start their own vegetable gardens for the hungry. Katie also received **grants** to help buy seeds. By 2011, Katie had established six gardens in her community. Katie would like to see gardens like hers providing food to hungry people everywhere.

This is one of six gardens that Katie sponsors in her home town.

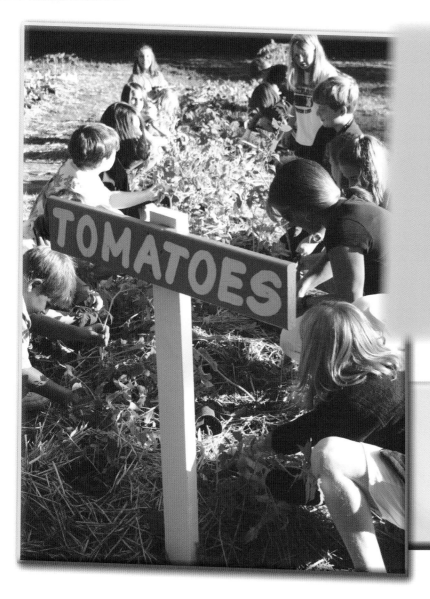

In their own words

Katie says, "My advice is to follow your heart. If you find a cause you truly believe in, you should do your best to help and you will make others happy as well as yourself. Doing something to help others makes your heart happy!"

Katie's entire school helps to plant, harvest, and distribute food from the school garden.

Kids who made a difference

In 1946, when Asfaw Yemiru was nine years old, he began living on the streets of Addis Ababa, Ethiopia's capital city. A kind woman took him in and sent him to school. Aged 14, Asfaw began teaching other poor children to read. By the time he was 17, over 200 children attended his lessons. Eventually, Asfaw raised money for school buildings and supplies. His free schools have educated thousands of poor children.

Katie is committed to helping the hungry, but she knows she cannot solve this problem alone. Her family and classmates help plant, weed, and harvest vegetables. Lisa Turocy, a master gardener, gives Katie gardening advice. Turocy says, "If I can help her change the world, that's awesome."

Spreading the word

Katie's project, like her garden, continues to grow. In 2011, Katie planned to offer two grants to young gardeners, but over 200 applied. Katie received so many great proposals, that she increased the number to seven full grants and three smaller grants. Katie has won several awards for her efforts, but she says that the greatest reward comes from helping others.

Top tips

Even if you can't grow your own garden, you can help feed the hungry. Why not collect tinned food for a **food bank** or participate in a fundraising event? Some food organizations need volunteers to sort food items and pack them for delivery. Soup kitchens often need volunteers to prepare and serve meals. Find what works best in your own community.

To learn more about her project, visit Katie's website at www.katieskrops.com.

Helping fight hunger

According to the World Hunger Organization, 925 million people around the world suffered from hunger in 2010. That's one out of every seven people. Children are at the greatest risk. Poor nutrition can cause learning disabilities, poor health, blindness, and death. About 5 million children die each year from causes related to hunger.

In May 2010, children in Paris, France participated in a race to raise money to help feed people in need.

Salim Sheikh: mapping the slum

Salim Sheikh and his friends worked for over a year to put their community on the map. Salim lives in the Rishi Aurobindo Colony, a community in Kolkata, India. Kolkata has one of the world's largest **slums**, with a population of about 1.5 million people. Rishi Aurobindo Colony is located within the slum.

Salim lives in Kolkata, a city in eastern India.

BHUTAN
CHINA
NEPAL
New Delhi
BANGLADESH
Kolkata
MYANMAR
INDIA
N
Mumbai
Bay of Bengal
Bangalore
INDIAN OCEAN
SRI LANKA
0   500 miles
0   500 kilometres

Slums are heavily populated, run-down sections of cities. About one in three city dwellers lives in a slum. Most slums lack basic services such as running water, electricity, and rubbish collection. Slum houses are often unsafe and crowded closely together. As more and more of the world's people move to cities, the number of people living in slums will increase.

Giving young people a voice

In the past, slums were not included on city maps. Officials ignored India's slums. Salim's maps show overcrowded conditions and a lack of schools, hospitals, and other vital services. The maps help communities to identify the services they need.

Salim is participating in a **UNICEF** (the United Nations Children's Fund) programme called Awaaz Do (Speak Up). Awaaz Do gives young people an opportunity to improve their communities.

The students in Kolkata's slums worked in groups to gather information.

In their own words

Martin Luther King Jr, an American **civil rights** leader, once said, "Everybody can be great. Because anybody can serve. You don't have to have a college degree to serve . . . You only need a heart full of grace. A soul generated by love."

Doing research

Salim worked in a team with three other young people. Each team included a photographer, note-takers, and a mapmaker. At each home, they asked:

* how many people live in the home?
* how old are they?
* what work do they do?
* do they have any particular health problems?

They made notes and photographed water pumps, crowded alleys, trees, temples, schools, and power sources.

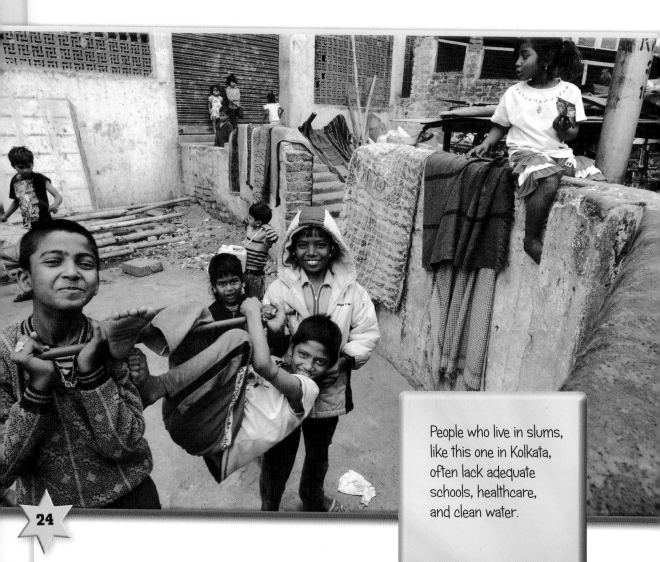

People who live in slums, like this one in Kolkata, often lack adequate schools, healthcare, and clean water.

After they gathered the information, Salim and his group created colourful, hand-drawn maps. The maps will be uploaded to Google Earth so that everyone can learn about Rishi Aurobindo Colony.

In their own words

Salim says, "With this map, everyone in the world will know we are here. We are a community with many issues and ideas, just like anybody."

Getting results

After Salim and his friends completed their maps, community leaders showed the maps to local officials. They used the maps to discuss particular problems in the slum. For example, the maps identified 71 water sources, but not a single one was safe for drinking. The maps provided community leaders with the proof they needed to convince city officials of their problems. Salim hopes that the maps will lead to improvements.

Top tips

Is there a problem in your community that is being ignored? If so, consider taking photos, writing an essay, or talking to an official about it. Children's voices can make a huge difference!

Using photography to help

Maps gave Salim a voice. In several other countries, students use photography to help their communities. UNICEF supplies the cameras and encourages young people to take pictures of particular problems. Some young people, like 17-year-old Shuktara Khatun, who lives in Bangladesh, take photos of young children who are working long hours in dangerous jobs. Fifteen-year-old Amadou Keita has taken photographs of working children in the West African country of Mali.

Sixteen-year-old Theresia (holding camera) photographs her community in the Central African Republic.

In their own words

Chadni Akther, aged 14, participated in the photography project in Bangladesh. She said, "Through pictures, I can tell the story of my hardships and the hardships of other children."

Many of the volunteers are children who live and work on the streets. The young people enjoy learning photography. The photos are a powerful tool for change. UNICEF displays the photographs in the cities where the young photographers live, and in special exhibitions in major cities, such as Tokyo and New York.

Kids who made a difference

In 1987, four-year-old Iqbal Masih (right) was forced to work in a carpet factory in Pakistan for 12 to 14 hours a day. If he refused to work, he was beaten. He escaped when he was 10 and began speaking about the terrible conditions faced by child **slaves** like himself. Iqbal's speeches brought worldwide attention to this problem and helped free hundreds of child workers. Very sadly, on 16 April 1995, 12-year-old Iqbal was murdered because of his courageous efforts to help the world's working children.

Ashlee Smith: bringing comfort

Ashlee Smith knows how it feels to lose everything. When she was six years old, a fire damaged Ashlee's home. All her toy horses, cuddly toys, and books had to be thrown out because of severe smoke damage. Ashlee felt sad and depressed. Two years later, Ashlee's experience and the news of another fire spurred her to action.

Ashlee's dad was a firefighter. In 2007, when Ashlee was eight, her dad and other firefighters were fighting the Angora Fire in nearby South Lake Tahoe. He sent pictures on his mobile phone that showed burned toys and melted tricycles. "I knew how those kids felt, and I just wanted to make a difference," said Ashlee. She began collecting toys to replace the things that the children had lost in the fire.

Ashlee lives in Sparks, Nevada, in the United States.

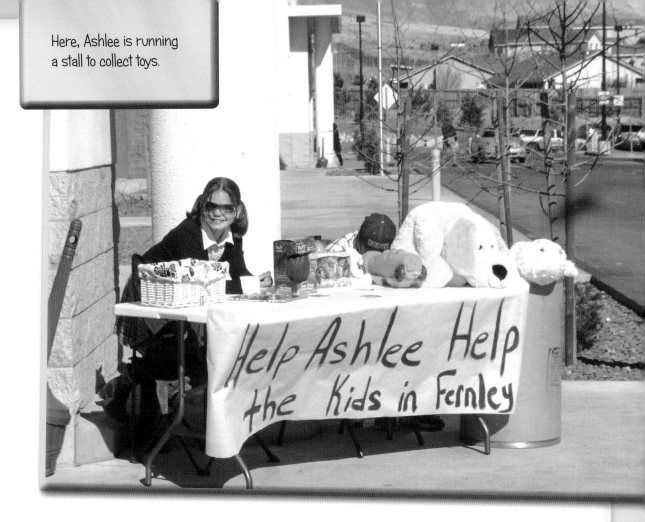

Here, Ashlee is running a stall to collect toys.

Helping kids

Ashlee's mother told her that other things were more important than toys. But Ashlee disagreed. She saw the problem from a child's point of view, and toys are important to children. Several organizations provided food and shelter. They worked with the adults, but Ashlee wanted to focus on the children. "I just feel like kids sometimes get put to the side; kids have feelings and are depressed about what's happened, too," she said. Ashlee began contacting local radio stations and asking people to contribute toys.

In their own words
Former British prime minister Winston Churchill once said, "We make a living by what we get, but we make a life by what we give."

Helping one child at a time

Within a few weeks of the Angora Fire, Ashlee had collected thousands of toys. When she began handing them out, Ashlee noticed one small girl reaching for a particular puzzle. It was exactly like one she had lost in the fire. The little girl's smile convinced Ashlee that she was doing something of value for children who had suffered losses. She was making a difference!

Ashlee's dream got bigger. She stood outside shops asking for **donations**, she spoke on local radio programmes, and she created flyers telling people about her project. By 2010, she had given over 175,000 toys to children who had lost their homes to fires, floods, or other natural disasters.

Ashlee's dad's work as a firefighter helped inspire her project, which she called "Ashlee's Toy Closet".

Helpful strangers

Ashlee's hard work brought rewards. She was featured in magazine and newspaper articles. She appeared on national television programmes. Ashlee used her newfound fame to expand her programme. People sent contributions from all over the country. Toy companies donated toys, and **haulage companies** offered to deliver toys to disaster areas. Ashlee has been amazed by the kindness and generosity of strangers who are eager to help. She thanks her family, too, and the neighbours who continue to support her.

Ashlee says that cuddly toys and books are favourites among the kids she helps.

In their own words

When asked to give advice to other young people, Ashlee said, "It's not that difficult. You can make a huge difference in someone's life by touching just one person's heart. It makes the world a better place."

Moving ahead

Just like Katie Stagliano set up her own charity, Katie's Krops, Ashlee also established a non-profit organization. Her website, Ashlee's Toy Closet, keeps **contributors** informed of her latest projects, needs, and sponsors. In addition to helping children in her own state, Ashlee has expanded her programme to other areas of the United States and the world. In 2010, Ashlee collected funds to help rebuild three **orphanages** in Haiti that had been destroyed in an earthquake. She also offers toys to parents who cannot afford to buy birthday gifts for their children.

Top tips

Sharing is great, but no one wants broken and dirty items. When you contribute toys, clothes, or other items to people in need, send things that are in good condition. New is best, but gently used is fine, too. Sometimes it is most helpful to send money so that people can buy what they really need.

To learn more about her project, visit Ashlee's website at www.ashleestoycloset.org.

In the spring of 2011, Ashlee began collecting toys for children in Joplin, Missouri, after a tornado destroyed homes there. Ashlee believes that with every toy, she also hands out hope. She wants children to know that they have not been forgotten.

When a tornado struck Joplin, Missouri, Ashlee began collecting toys for children who lost everything.

In their own words

Bishop Desmond Tutu won the Nobel Peace Prize in 1984 for his efforts to bring peace to his nation of South Africa. He once said, "Do your little bit of good where you are: it's those little bits of good put together that overwhelm the world."

Ryan Hreljac: providing clean water

In 1998, six-year-old Ryan Hreljac's teacher told him that people in faraway places were dying because they did not have clean water. Ryan decided to do something about it. His teacher said that a well would cost 70 Canadian dollars (about £26 at that time). Ryan asked his parents for the money, but they didn't give it to him. They made him earn it by doing extra jobs like washing windows and vacuuming the floors. It took him four months to earn $70.

Ryan grew up in Kemptville, Ontario, in Canada.

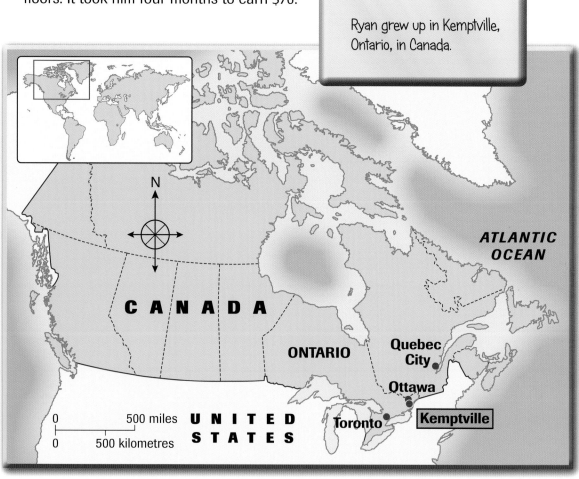

That's when Ryan learned that $70 would only buy the hand pump that sits on top of the well. A complete well would cost $2,000 (£750). So Ryan did more jobs. A local newspaper ran a story about Ryan's project, and people started sending donations. By January 1999, Ryan had enough money to pay for an entire well near a primary school in Agweo, Uganda.

The problem

While he was earning the money, Ryan learned more about water problems around the world. Nearly one in eight people do not have access to clean water. Every single day, about 4,500 children die from drinking unsafe water. Many others become ill or suffer poor health. Babies and children are in the greatest danger. In many areas of the world, children walk miles to collect water and the only water they can find is dirty.

In their own words
Albert Schweitzer, a German doctor who founded a medical clinic in West Central Africa, said, "Do something wonderful, people may imitate it."

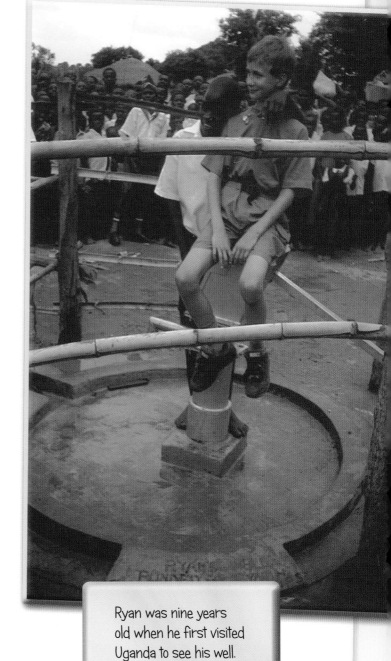

Ryan was nine years old when he first visited Uganda to see his well.

Speaking out

Ryan learned that digging wells by hand is difficult. For $25,000 (£9,500), he could buy a power drill that would make digging wells in Uganda quicker and simpler. To raise more money, Ryan began talking to school children about the need for clean water wells in Africa. The more Ryan spoke about his dream of providing clean water to the world, the more other children and adults joined the cause. Soon, Ryan's story appeared in national newspapers and on television.

When Ryan was nine, he visited his well in Agweo, Uganda. People greeted him with cheers. His well had made Agweo a healthier place. People now had clean water for drinking, cooking, and washing.

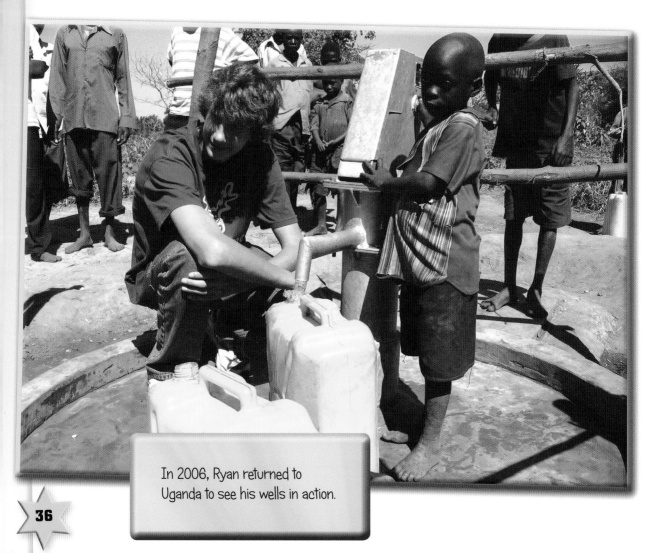

In 2006, Ryan returned to Uganda to see his wells in action.

Ryan's Well

In 2001, Ryan and his supporters created a non-profit organization called Ryan's Well **Foundation**. Ryan spoke all over the world. He not only raised money, but he taught people about the importance of clean water.

In addition to building wells, Ryan's foundation also teaches people how to take care of the well and how to keep water clean by building **latrines** (outdoor toilets) far from wells. By 2011, Ryan's Well Foundation had built wells and latrines that benefit 723,375 people in 16 different countries. Projects continue in several African countries and in Haiti.

Top tips

Ryan's Well Foundation is one of many organizations building wells around the world. Your contributions could help. Consider raising money for clean water, but make sure a parent checks out any organization before you send money. It is important to make sure the charity uses money wisely.

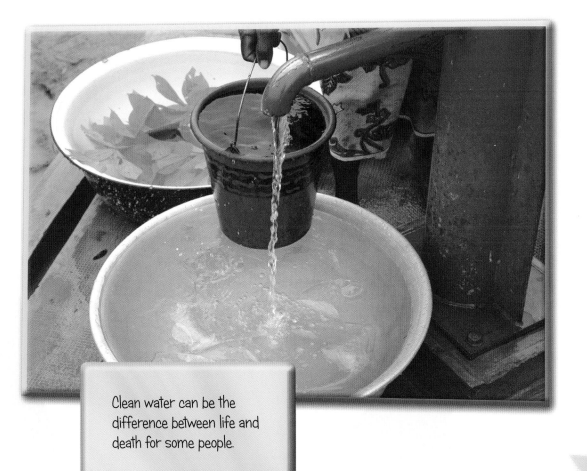

Clean water can be the difference between life and death for some people.

Person to person

Ryan not only helped to build wells and latrines, but he also connected with the people of Uganda. Ryan's teacher arranged for him and his classmates to write to children in Uganda. When Ryan visited in 2000, he met his pen pal, Jimmy Akana. The two boys became friends. When Ryan learned that Jimmy's life was in danger, Ryan and his family arranged to bring Jimmy to Canada. Jimmy became a brother to Ryan, and the boys continue to work together to help others.

A well that provides clean drinking water is important for keeping a community healthy.

Working together

Although Ryan worked hard, he could not have accomplished his goals alone. One of Ryan's aims is to motivate people to help others. Makenzie Conner, aged 17, wanted to help others, too. She worked with the Water Project. Like Ryan's Well, the Water Project is a non-profit organization that builds wells. In 2011, Makenzie, who lives in Michigan, USA, raised US$1,000 (£630) for The Water Project as part of a school assignment.

When a Year 4 pupil called Sam Decker read about Makenzie's success in the local newspaper, he called her and asked if she would help him raise money for clean water. Sam's teacher had given each student one dollar to "change the world". Mackenzie was happy to help. Sam used his dollar to make signs and cans for donations. He raised US$104 (£65). By working together, Makenzie and Sam made a difference!

To learn more about Ryan's Well Foundation, visit their website at www.ryanswell.ca.

Top tips

If you want to raise money for charity, set yourself a goal. For example, you might aim to raise £20, or maybe you think you could raise £100! Having a goal will keep you motivated to keep going until you reach your target.

You can make a difference

On his 17th birthday, pop star Justin Bieber asked family, friends, and fans to contribute US$17 (£10) in his honour to a clean water project in **developing nations**. "Even if you don't have US$17 to give," he told fans, "I just ask you to go out in your community and try and make a positive difference. Even the smallest act of kindness can go a long way." Over 2,000 fans raised US$47,544 (£29,800) for clean water.

You don't need to be famous to help others. Matt Pearce, Dionne Burns, and Jared Vigil were not famous. They used skills they had learned to help others in need. Katie Stagliano and Salim Sheikh learned the new skills of gardening and mapping to help their communities. Ashlee Smith and Ryan Hreljac learned about a particular problem and took steps to solve it. They had to raise money to reach their goals. Raising money is not easy, so it is not the right choice for everyone. What will you do to help? The choice is yours.

Talia Leman was 10 years old when she began helping others.

Kids who made a difference

Talia Leman was 10 years old in August 2005 when Hurricane Katrina destroyed thousands of homes in New Orleans and the surrounding area. Talia decided to help. She encouraged children all over the United States to "trick-or-treat for Katrina." They raised over US$ 10 million (£5.6 million). Talia wanted to do more so she started a project called RandomKid. It helps young people organize fundraising projects. Children and teenagers using Talia's website have raised money for hundreds of different projects.

These children are running a marathon in Ramallah, Palestine to raise money for local children's projects.

Making a difference map

Arctic Ocean

N

Ryan Hreljac (pages 34–39) lived in Kemptville, Ontario, Canada when he started his clean water project.

Jared Virgil (page 14) helped a neighbour in Louisville, Colorado, USA.

Ashlee Smith (pages 28–33) runs her toy charity from her home in Sparks, Nevada, USA.

NORTH

AMERICA

Atlantic Ocean

Katie Stagliano (pages 16–21) grows vegetables to feed the hungry in Summerville, South Carolina, USA.

SOUTH AMERICA

Pacific Ocean

0   3000 miles

0   3000 kilometres

Dionne Burns (page 12) helped save a life in Glasgow, Scotland.

Matt Pearce (pages 10–15) helped a stroke victim in Longlevens, England.

Salim Sheikh (pages 22–27) helped map his neighbourhood in Kolkata, India.

Chadni Akther (page 27) takes photos in Bangladesh to help improve children's lives.

Amadou Keita (page 26) takes photos in Mali to help child workers.

Tilly Smith (page 15) was on holiday in Phuket, Thailand, when she warned people about a tsunami.

Asfaw Yemiru (page 19) has set up schools in Addis Ababa, Ethiopia.

Ryan Hreljac's first well was dug in Uganda.

Arctic Ocean

ASIA

EUROPE

AFRICA

Pacific Ocean

AUSTRALASIA

Indian Ocean

Southern Ocean

ANTARCTICA

Tips on making a difference

Are you ready to help? If so, here are a few tips on what to do:

Find the right project for you

One way to help is to join a project that's already up and running. It is important to choose one that matches your interests, skills, and talents. If you truly believe in a project, it will be easier to commit your time and energy to it.

* Talk to friends, parents, and teachers. What organizations do they support? Why? Do any of their causes interest you?

* Watch for announcements at school or in the community about local charity events. Local organizations such as soup kitchens or children's hospitals often hold fundraising events and ask for volunteers.

Choosing a charity

It is important to research a charity before you donate your money or time. An adult can help you do this. Here are some tips:

* First, find a charity that helps a cause you are interested in. Websites such as www.charitychoice.co.uk allow you to search charities by topic.

* Find out how the charity uses its money. Does most of it go to the people who need it? There are websites listed on page 47 that can help you find out.

* Once you've chosen a charity, find out what help they need. Some are looking for volunteers, others for donations of money or goods.

Starting your own project

If you can't find the right project, you might want to start your own. This can be a big job, so don't be afraid to ask for help! Learn as much as you can about the problem you want to solve. Is there anyone else in your community or elsewhere who is working towards the same goals? You might be able to learn from them, or even get their support. Once you decide on a particular project, develop a plan to reach your goal.

Talk with a trusted adult

Many of the young people featured in this book had help and support from their parents and other trusted adults. You should discuss your idea with a parent, teacher, or club leader. An adult will help you stay safe. They can provide advice and check to see that any organization you want to help is worthy of your time and effort.

Involve others

Working together leads to success – there is strength in numbers! When starting a new project, try to find people who share your goals and will help you. You may be surprised at how eager your family, friends, and schoolmates are to lend a hand.

Glossary

charity organization that raises money for those in need

civil rights rights of people to be equal to others and have political and social freedom

community service project specific task designed to help others

contributor someone who gives money, goods, or help to a project

developing nation country where the average income is much lower than in industrial nations

diplomat government official who deals with foreign countries

donation gift of money, goods, or help to a person or project

dyke long wall or embankment built to stop flooding from the sea

first aid emergency medical care

First Lady wife of the US President

food bank charity that gives out donated food to the hungry

foundation organization that provides funds for charity

fundraise collect money for a specific project

grant sum of money provided for a specific project

haulage company company that transports goods

humanitarian person who works to improve human welfare

latrine toilet like a trench dug into the ground

moral teaching, lesson, or message

non-profit organization group that is not intended to make a profit, but is set up to provide a public service

nun woman who belongs to and lives with a religious group

observant quick to notice, alert

orphanage place that houses and cares for children who do not have parents

paramedic emergency medical worker or doctor

recycle treat or process materials so that they can be used again

slave person who works for another without pay or rights

slum heavily populated, run-down section of a city

soup kitchen place where food is served at little or no cost to the needy

sponsor give money or help to a charity or good cause. A company or organization that helps support a particular project is called a sponsor.

symptom sign of a medical problem

tsunami unusually large sea wave produced by an earthquake or undersea volcanic eruption

UNICEF (United Nations Children's Fund) a United Nations organization devoted to the needs of children throughout the world

Find out more

Books

101 Ways to be a Hero, Charlotte Guillain (Raintree, 2011)

Kids Care!: 75 Ways to Make a Difference for People, Animals and the Environment, Rebecca Olien (Williamson Books, 2007)

Overseas Twinning, Sally Hewitt (Franklin Watts, 2006)

Ryan and Jimmy and the Well in Africa that Brought Them Together, Herb Shoveller (Kids Can Press, 2006)

Take Your Best Shot, Austin Gutwein and Todd Hillard (Thomas Nelson, 2009)

Websites

Visit The Water Project at **thewaterproject.org**

To investigate possible ways of helping others through RandomKid, visit **www.randomkid.org**

Learn more about UNICEF at **www.unicef.org**

Find a charity you can trust on the GuideStar website at **www.guidestar.org.uk**

Visit **www.junction49.co.uk** – an online forum for young people to share ideas about helping others.

The Charity Commission regulates charities in the UK. Visit their website at **www.charity-commission.gov.uk** to find information on charities and their projects, and to learn about setting up your own.

At **www.charitychoice.co.uk** you can search for charities by name or by category.

Index